The ramblings of an anxious mind

Debbie Edgar-Bowers

Presentation by *BookLeaf Publishing*

Web: www.bookleafpub.com

E-mail: info@bookleafpub.com

ISBN: 978-93-5761-091-9

First edition 2022

DEDICATION

My husband David who is always by my side.
My parents Susan and Bill who are supportive
in everything I do.

ACKNOWLEDGEMENT

The inspiration for my writing is taken from Franz Kafka and Anne Sexton. Their words are absolute perfection.

Rain on an Autumn day

Day is never getting brighter
Dark clouds and raindrops spilling
Gloomy people rushing around
As if the world is falling apart
Sit down for a moment
Appreciate the goodness
Plants and flowers being watered
Farmers crops soaking it up
Wild animals having a drink
Pitter patter on the windows
The greatest sound doesn't cost a penny
Brollies and wellies all part of the fun
Splashing in puddles making mud
It's only water
Just embrace it
Without rain there are never rainbows

Crafters Paradise

Glitter and sequins, everywhere
Piles of paper, stacks of card
Stickers and toppers, washi tapes too
Unorganised mess, what a delight
Glitter and sequins, everywhere
Cutting mats, craft knives
Needle and thread, fabric and pins
Patchwork and embroidery, anything goes
Glitter and sequins, everywhere
Paint splashes, marker pens
A blank canvas for the mind
Nothing in order, the perfect space
Glitter and sequins, everywhere

The Darkness

I'm just a person walking around
The Darkness following without a sound
Day after day, night after night
Bad thoughts filling my head
Happy or sad I wish I could choose
Fed up of feeling like I've nothing to lose
Put a smile on the outside, no one will know
My mind full of Darkness, don't put it on show
Good things to come, I'm trying to focus
Because no matter what I'll always beat this

Bibliophile

See the world through different eyes
Visit every country in the world
Feet up at the sofa or comfy on the beach
A cup of tea, a coffee and a piece
On holiday, commuting, anything goes
Travel through time or outer space
Take every single page at your own pace
A memoir, poetry, fiction or fact
Learning new words and things to share
A book is the tunnel to everywhere

Three beautiful red roses

Bright red petals glistening
Shiny and as bright as tears
Clutched in tiny hands minding the thorns
Thrown into the ground with a sad smile
A small piece of each of us with you
Three beautiful red roses
Six feet underground

Anxiety

Every single day, the feeling of dread
Wondering if this will ever end
Did I smile back, what words did I use?
How did they respond, was it okay?
Every little thought over and over
Twisting and turning, my stomach is churning
Fast beating heart trying to slow down
Counting to ten, learning to breathe
And on with my day, nothing to see here

The Dream

Closing my eyes as darkness descends
Will he return when I give in to sleep
Fighting the tiredness to keep him away
Exhaustion will win every time
Here he is, night by night
A constant reminder of a day not so bright
Wake up with a start, a fast beating heart
It's only a memory, go back to sleep
My mind will always be stronger than my
emotions

Memories

Days at the beach running around
Swimming in the water, dunking my brother
Cucumber sandwiches covered in sand
Staying in a caravan all cosy and sound
Winning in the arcades, games before bed
Ice creams for everyone, what a treat
Candy floss, rock, a few souvenirs
A postcard or two to send to our friends
Loving every moment right up to the end

Bread and Honey

Evenings playing coiny watching trash on tv
Balloons stuck to the ceiling making me laugh
Friday night sleepovers just you and me
Watching the wrestling eating our tea
Bowling, arcades, football matches in Liverpool
Our special movie, peas, carrots and chocolate
Teaching me swear words not to tell mum
Chasing away bad guys in my dreams
Always around and eager to please
Here if you need me, a shout as he leaves
Need you now, an instant reply

Tired Tired Tired

So tired of effort
And faking a smile
No one to notice the sadness
Head crammed full of badness
Tired of pretending to be okay
Just carrying on with the day
Tired of fighting and never winning
Enough to make your head start spinning
Tired of trying but always failing
Always second never the best
Wanting to be treated like all the rest
Tired of breathing
Tired of living

School days

Skipping in the playground
Swapping snacks after class
Playing rounders and football
Pogs, yo-yos and cricket
Conkers and acorns free fun for all
Simple fun but we had a ball
Lunchtime gossip with my friends
Making plans for the weekend
Those days were the days
Everyone was my friend

Sidekick

Plaiting my hair, counting to 100
Eager to leave, toys to be played with
Matching perms, smiles and attitudes
There for each other without a doubt
Taking me shopping, buying me books
My small legs struggling to keep up
Days at the park, picnics in the woods
Now I'm a grown up (they say!)
Doesn't mean I don't need you every single day
Driving me around, always supporting
Crafting and organising, watering my plants
My mum, my sidekick, always by my side

Dogs

A paw on my leg or a head by my feet
Following me around until I take a seat
A long day at work, a slow journey home
Forgotten at once seeing their face
A bark of excitement and a lick of glee
Quick little rub, a treat or three
Showing their affection, nothing to hide
Always so happy just to be by my side

Halloween Halloween Halloween

Blood orange pumpkins carved into shapes
The darkest black bats flying so high
Spiders as big as can be
Vampires on the hunt, ghouls making me jump
Beautiful witches casting spells
Wizards and monsters everywhere
Trick or treat, given me a fright
Cauldrons and fangs, blood and guts
Children having fun, oh what a sight

Cookie

15

Love is more than a word
So easy to say
To feel in your heart
And mean it each day
The distance was hard
But here you will stay
I loved you before I met you
I assure you that's true
Stronger together side by side
Even when I want to hide
You're my rock when life is hard
Every problem we will get through
Just remember I love you

A hug

Hello or goodbye
A touch of sadness
A flutter of happiness
Safe and secure, to show you care
Feeling loved and needed
Cared for and wanted
A quick little squeeze
Or a long one with ease
Your choice to make however you please
A giant squeeze of emotions

Distance

17

What's a little distance between friends
Countless miles, so far apart
So many years, so many calls
Wondering if I'll see you at all
My very best friend, like family to me
Whatever happens, don't doubt me
One day again, reunited you'll see
I love you my friend
My twin forever

Gone fishing

Just a man and his dog
A quiet day on the river
Box full of tackle, bag full of dinner
The great outdoors
Enjoying every moment
His black lab beside him
The most faithful best friend
Catching fish to share at the end
Just a man and his dog
Forever fishing

www.ingramcontent.com/pod-product-compliance
Lightning Source LLC
LaVergne TN
LVHW021354200726

843509LV00014B/2836

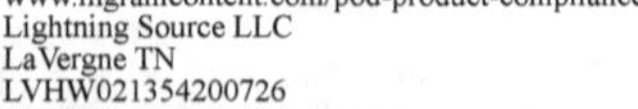